WHILE SUPPLIES LAST

While Supplies Last

ANITA LAHEY

Signal EDITIONS

THE POETRY IMPRINT AT VÉHICULE PRESS

Published with the generous assistance of the Canada Council for the Arts and the Canada Book Fund of the Department of Canadian Heritage.

SIGNAL EDITIONS EDITOR: CARMINE STARNINO

Cover design by David Drummond
Photograph of author by Colin Rowe
Set in Minion and Filosofia by Simon Garamond
Printed by Marquis Book Printing Inc.

Dépôt légal, Library and Archives Canada and the Bibliothèque national du Québec, second trimester 2023

LIBRARY AND ARCHIVES CANADA CATALOGUING IN PUBLICATION

Title: While supplies last / Anita Lahey.
Names: Lahey, Anita, author.
Description: Poems.
Identifiers: Canadiana (print) 20220497249 | Canadiana (ebook) 20220497257 | ISBN 9781550656220 (softcover) | ISBN 9781550656299 (EPUB)
Classification: LCC PS8623.A393 W55 2023 | DDC C811/.6—dc23

Published by Véhicule Press, Montréal, Québec, Canada
vehiculepress.com

Distribution in Canada by LitDistCo
litdistco.ca

Distribution in the U.S. by Independent Publishers Group
ipgbook.com

Printed in Canada on FSC certified paper.

For all who look, marvel, and fret

it's enough to record
what's obvious,
here in the foreground.

but always this is what's
hardest to see

—JOHN STEFFLER,
The Grey Islands

Contents

Seasonal Affective Disorder

Pandemic Traffic Reports

The Great Fire of Main-à-Dieu

Songs for Main-à-Dieu

Seasonal Affective Disorder

Overnight Tsunami Warning Lifted

Tide's out. It came
and went before we woke.
The low-lying spit

with its bracelet of stones
cradles the bay. Waves fizz
and firs bow

under histories stored
in needle and bark. Mountains
rearrange their glistening

shawls. A layer sloughs
off and wedges in where
no light falls. Signals

drift over rooftops, dew,
filter into the wrong ears, sound
too late. We're each

adding our bit
to the undersea pile-on.
Someday—will any of us

be here, waiting?—
a sigh from earth's core
will jet-stream it all back out.

Preparation's a mere
to-do list away.

Salish Sea (with Crows)

Gulls call carnage. Fish
head. Crab carcass. Every
tide, this brilliant toss
reassembles. Seaweeds

drape barnacles and grit,
tangled and glistening
like ruined violin strings,
a sea serpent's sperm

(you name it). Meanwhile,
offshore, freighters float,
shrouded in mist. I can't
reconcile the dignity

these ships convey with
the goofy octopus t-shirts
and sushi-shaped erasers
joggling their stores. I turn

my eye to the crows. I live
among them now, the original
beachcombers, poking and sifting,
discarding a clam shell here,

skirting a puddled jellyfish
there. The whole arrangement's
sprinkled with plastic
chips sunnier than

a yellowlegs' legs, more
profanely orange
than the oystercatcher's bill—
Mornings, evenings, here

they come, tide
out, tide in, by wing, by foot,
these spry devils, snickering
and scheming.

The Moon and the City

There's always a shortcut
we haven't mapped. A language
for every block. A no-go zone
in a park. Strange matter

on the flipside
of a wall: bookcase,
baby, dog, dust, a painting
you'll never encounter

but imagine while lying
on the floor, walking
your bare feet up
and down the plaster.

Between earth and roof,
a wavering squirrel digs
eighteen toes into brick. Higher,
through its half-lidded

eye, the moon indulges
streetlamps. It tugs
the loose parts
inside us. Sparrows

spray from a hedge, arguing
brightly. Raccoons peer,
consider the odds. Crows
commandeer laneways. They

organize wakes. A crime's
underway, kitchen fires, death—
Someone's put coffee on.
A cluster of daisies

passes through a door. Love,
too, and a boy crashing
laughing into bed.
We're drawn,

blinking, to hushed
evening assemblies. Railings,
rust. Bats slice the dusk. We
never all sleep at once.

Seasonal Affective Disorder

An altered season's
having her way
with every shapely

cloud. She's got all
this stuff to throw at us:
midnight furies, fervour

and floods, white-hot
rends in afternoon skies.
Summer's never been

so cumulo-
nimbus-charmed.
She blows

through the window, simmering
bodies to a salt broth—
Wouldn't we

fall over ourselves
to be like that, devastating,
once in our lives?

Urgent Interspecies Telepathy
in a Sunlit Bedroom

for Maureen

The chickadee's wings blur
over bed and lamp, missing
with each dash-and-swoop
the turnoff back to its foliage-
garlanded sky. On a nearby nail,
two carved dolphins leap
toward open air. It's

no use. Drop three
pennies in your hand: a third
of an ounce, this off-course
aviator. I worry for its heart
knocking the glass (500 beats
per minute in repose), recali-
brating with each collision
the validity of sight. It'd be
so great to say to this
panicked creature, *I'm sorry*

you're scared, I know what it means
to be a fish out of water—see it
shake a few feathers, chirp
at the misplaced
metaphor. I close my
eyes and will the bird

to pause: please allow
the daylight drifting in
to slip beneath a wingtip,
whisper the angle
by which to whoosh
out and away.

January Wasn't For the Faint of Heart

The atmosphere around me
has a different saturation point
than it does for moms who post primers
on sweet-potato mash. Over here,

the actual newspaper, ink on fingers,
double-page spread of six-pointed
crystals. Snowflakes shapeshift
according to the temperature

and humidity along their drift, variable
even for two falling
side-by-side,
lifelong—

Before racers, saucers and McDonald's trays,
people used cookie sheets, plastic bags,
sheets of cardboard. In the warm
layer under snow, mice

burrow tunnels. Deeper
still are ferns. They'll pop up
in spring—fiddleheads!—& we'll all
be excited: that feathery swirl,

the end of snowflakes
for a time. I'll tell you
a little about ferns
while they sleep. A fern

flower on the eve of the Feast
of St. John the Baptist:
happiness is yours. A fern
may help you locate hidden

treasure. One fern-crazed Victorian
invented a glass box
to protect his garden
from London's smog. The air

was fouled by coal, and the substance
of coal includes the fossils
of ancient ferns. Did Dr. Ward
grasp this irony? His Wardian case

led to terrariums and aquariums
and perhaps the idea that plants
and other living things
are fragile—

we'd best keep them
under wraps. We should all be
tucked into glazed domes,
before things get

out of hand. Fingerprints,
frost, clouded glass. Tendrils
brushing. Out there, tiny
flames may continue

to trace
unrepeatable
paths. Everything
alters enroute.

Hydro Pylons, All in a Row

Their bones, once molten,
edge nothingness
and smog.

You know them as all the lost limbs from
darkest times redeployed—landmine, crash, drone-fire rubble
snapped together. Earth's arteries liquefied, scorched, remade
to brave connection. Sentries   with sharp-edged shoulders
steeled against the flood,   they balance parcels of sky

with storm
clouds stuffed in,
spilling over—
They exude
a skeletal grace. Crows

veer that way, cawing, through blue
cutouts like remnants of clarity—flattened, scissored, hemmed.
Consider their open-heart triangles

through which fish leap unseen   at windless 2 a.m.'s. Bolted,
coiled, humming, ankle-deep   in snowmelt ponds, they direct
& re-direct the current. They bring   light, whistling kettles, messages
from far-off friends. They pass   night shadows and warmth
endlessly forward. They relay   that surge we live by—

Neither Here Nor There

Not in Burlington, where the lake's boarded up
with caged boulders and e. coli warnings.
Flocks of geese cross the road on foot,
single-file (braked cars huff and puff).

Not across the Don, where I adopted
a kitten, the pipes burst and I spent
evenings on sidewalks peering in
at bookshelves, chandeliers, families.

Nor Ottawa, where, when weariness struck
I'd nestle into the nearest snow bank
with a tea-stained copy of *The Heat of the Day*, or pretend
to be safe and sound in the Diefenbunker.

There was once Montreal, where riderless
bicycles roll up winding staircases and potholes
square-dance under full moons. (In spring, near the fountain
in the park, papier-maché politicians bloom.)

Outside Krakow, farms harbour hiding holes
and execution sites, tracks hum forgetfully
and tomatoes hang amid Hail Marys, red and heavy
and whole. My people left there decades ago.

A half-breath in Fredericton, where the mayor'd been
mayor since the ice house held ice, where pretty homes
with painted shingles cascade shadows over elms,
crows and poets, down to the Saint John's shore.

There's no going back to Nan's bog-patched
Cape Breton village that burned then burst back up, only
to lose hold of one child after another: they left (like Dad)
in a hurry, as if they were being smoked out.

Not here, either, beneath streaking gulls and 737s,
our barn-style roof, the locust's teardrop leaves.
Here, absorbed in humidity, tending our transplanted
peony, noting the faint subway rumble downstairs.

A Pair, Fishing the Humber

In the shallows, sleek white feathers,
stick-thin stillness, sudden death. Mid-stream:
smooth black waders, lures and tangles,
Muskol dreams. Up to their knees

in the rushing from the weir's
rainbow trout jumps and sea lamprey
detection cage—webbing, boot soles—
each senses the other. The bird

and the man didn't meet
on the reinforced bank, trade in
Hurricane Hazel souvenirs, share
tackle and bait. They breathe

an atmosphere of do-gooders
and bank-shorers, invasive-species
armies, flood-plain swat teams,
the recitations of amateur

historians—
this pulsing, off-key, post-contact
aftermath. Heartache zeroes in
from the lookoffs—

sighs of a Haudenosaunee harvest,
ice jams and drowning dogs. Ever see
a trout make it up those ladders?
(I'm told when the water's

sufficiently high, it's a cinch.)
The current pools below
the footbridge. Love's padlocks
bubble with rust. Cormorants

loiter on moored concrete,
oily wings open, ghoul-heads
bowed. A night heron
sleeps it off

in the branchery. On numbing
legs, he sways, resists
the river's pull. Could it
(the mallard-littered

maw) seal off
in silt and despair?
A kingfisher dashes
through dankness

under Bloor, comes up
with a beakful. That egret
gangles the shoreline. Twitches
to a flashing.

High Park Welcoming Bird

for Xiaomin and the Scarlet Tanager

My friend eyed a wonder
in the branchy riot: a bird
red as the devil's eye.
We were halfway down
a stairway calling up
ghosts through ravines.
Craning, frowning—
this was no cardinal—
we studied the guide, flitting
from sketches and notes
to that mystery perched.

A proper ID's a gathering
of clues: habitat, habit, shape.
A breeder's plumage pops,
then fades. The wings
were black as a nun's sleeve,
tail a swatch of night, radiating
stars and dew. The red bird
crooked its thin toes over bark,
held itself to itself, like a child
dreaming a vision she
can't explain. Mapping
a flight? Wishing us

gone. I'm flailing between
curiosity, gratitude and deep,
cosmic dismay. That bird,

a plump cherry, say, a crimson
heart, flight feathers on standby,
rosy head atilt. We basked
in its surprising warmth,
we oohed, we breathed, and Christ,
how hard we looked. At length,
we ruled out every rival, offered up
a name. And from this faraway
dream, I invoke it again.

Saskatoon Berries by Value Village

for Sherry

Uphill from the Saint John, a building expels
bargain seekers into wind, ice, dark. They flounder
between cars, bulging with bags. A woman
slinks the riparian zone that buffers

this sea of cheap finds (dishware,
cardigans, coats) muttering *You can't
have them all!* at haughty
cedar waxwings. Out here,

amid the mangy greenery
that edges parking lots everywhere,
branches poke. A chorus of beaks
berates. She's crouched, fingers

flashing. Serviceberries. Shadbush.
The picking's hypnotic. She's known
to swish hangers in cluttered aisles,
frown over frayed cuffs, hangdog

boots. Deals cluster. Treasures
burst to be plucked. Burdened shoppers
trail the waning day. Motors
cough and spit, vibrating

a subzero wind. Her eyes
sting. Myths ripen (witches,
whatnot). You might call them
Juneberries. Amazing

they're so plentiful
this late in the season. Her bowl
brims. Satisfaction deepens
and plumps. One day

only. All this juicy, nutty
sweetness. While supplies last.

Sparrows Everywhere

In a May dusk lilac drunk
outside the curry house
I sidestep

a splay of filth
on the sidewalk, a crumpled
wrapper someone tossed.

Closer up, the blot
unblurs into extremities,
a miniscule leg

askew, dust-encrusted feathers
fanning off a wing bone
torqued to an acute

angle. The beak's
—yes, a beak!—cranked
open on the concrete

like a grotesque miniature
cradling its portion
of atmosphere.

The bright day
this block was poured,
a worker under hot sun

brushed the wet cement
with a stiff broom to score
shallow ridges. Three thin toes

radiate over them now,
framed in sprightly weeds. It's true,
we have sparrows

everywhere. Railings, mulch beds,
sills. The cedars we shape into
walls are alive

with swashbucklers
poised to lift and ruffle
the higher aspects. Their bold

trajectories, their swoop
and veer, remind me of sparklers
grasped in sweaty hands

that one night each spring
we go giddy and expansive
in our bid to outdo

the stars. That night
of crackles and whistling
is nearly upon us.

Ice-Age Surprise

1.

The baby mammoth strayed a foot too far.
A mud-slick pool claimed one leg, one more,
she tipped and kicked and sank before
the females in the herd could crowbar
her onto their teeming tundra's safe, hard
ground. The beasts lumbered off toward
sedges, sagebrush, shrubs, the score
one down for a species doomed. The star
of this exhibit pierced the permafrost
snow-encrusted, petrified, a wince
sunk into her pose. She's crossed
all those eons—are we convinced
by her stiff, drab folds? We lean in, exhale.
Her trunk, curled, enfolds the gale.

2.

Her trunk, curled, enfolds a gale
of long-lost terror let loose in tremolo.
She thrashes, gasps, writhes with immense
cries and roars against the undertow. . .
that slurping, all-consuming down-suck. The bed
of the Yuribei bulges. Cracks. Stills
its catch. An ice-bound secret pickles
in the sediment of her habitat. Instead
of ducking spears, swipes from sabre-tooth cats,
lumbering into adulthood with the herd,
she ferments in soil, acid, time—intact.
That mud choked and drowned and made her *were*.
Yet she *is*: shrivelled to half her heft,
transformed, preserved, what's left.

3.

Transformed, preserved, what's left
from her thirty-two days of life includes
her whole heart plus skin, bones, lungs, tufts
of thick brown mammoth hair—and food,
the last meal of a baby giant pooled
in her X-rayed gut. Milk, of course.
In her winding intestine, remnants of stool,
Mama Mammoth its likeliest source,
her feces sowing microbes for a someday
eater of plants. But Lyuba never dined
on broad-leafed herbs. The steppe's buffet
of windswept grass rustled her infant mind.
Proboscidean eyelashes delight.
Milk tusks shy from the gallery's light.

4.

Milk tusks shy from the gallery's light;
its dimness cradles a bent-back hoof,
a wrinkle-nestled eye shut tight.
She's fossil, mystery, rune, aloof—
our specimen of life gone still.
We'll set queries to the rings on her tusks,
to her hump of fat apply a drill,
lay bare her bones, run scans and bask
in theories of how she lived and died.
Say she dodged a hyena, then tumbled.
Wandered, a toddler, from Mama's side.
I've been sucked right into this fumble
for clues, a plot, redemption. What more?
She's 42,000 years old. On tour.

5.

She's 42,000 years old, on tour
from the Late Pleistocene to Chicago,
a Siberian sandbar to Salekhard,
Sydney, St. Petersburg, Tokyo.
An underworld beast breaks ground!
Is this it? The deities' reprimand?
Ivory's coveted, traders abound.
You know? I can almost understand
what drove the cousin to steal the corpse—
a year's supply of grub, a snowmobile
or two. Propped against Novvy Port's
main-drag shop, she gave up her tail
to a hungry dog, an ear to a similar cause.
Phones, flickering, clustered like stars.

6.

Phones, flickering, clustered like stars
come to earth in that far-north town,
converging and refracting, pulsars
beating *wtf. No way.* And *Wow.*
(That is, however astonishment's
conveyed in the lingo here.) As to ice,
I wonder what's said—on, say, the punishment
of these mild winters. Their price?
Reindeer crossings and sled-friendly roads
to edible growth. A muddy hunger
thickens, boosts the weight of their loads.
What rites exist for casting asunder
all hopes for seasonal comforts, predictable skies?
It could serve as consolation, this surprise.

7.

Could it serve as consolation, this surprise?
Our sole reward for catastrophic thaw:
one nearly perfect beast to mythologize.
Imagine ice-age matriarchal law,
the buds they plucked with delicate, dexterous
tips of trunks. We fashioned combs,
built durable huts; made daggers, spatulas;
mistook their tusks for dragons' bones,
believed they rumbled and burrowed below,
perished if sun or moonlight struck
their monstrous, hairy hides. I know
this ivory woman, bird, those killing sticks
(boomerang-curved). Atop a deep-dug grave,
mourners positioned a shoulder blade.

8.

Mourners positioned a shoulder blade
over two dead infants long ago.
They chose with care, they were afraid
of scavengers, the spirit world. Snow
and ice piled over that site, till the cold
bone warmed and twitched and cast
off the hard layers of time. If I fold
these phrases over her limbs, will they last
forty more millennia? By then
dry winds may shush through grass,
birds serenade a steppe that again
wends placidly north, on past
the site of an animal's fall
through time. I sputter and stall.

Don River: Crossings and Expeditions

1.

A worker honey bee
from the abandoned apiary
in the cottage backyard of famed naturalist Charles Sauriol
motors over the riverbank and plunges
into a wall of black swallowwort. One more
newfangled post-industrial invader. (It straitjackets
trees and strangles dogs.) Bring this mighty forager
a blossom all native and nectar-y, bring it
a highrise of goldenrod, an eighteenth-century
bustle of milkweed. On the double. (Where
is the ghost of Elizabeth Simcoe
when you need her?)

2.

A skate blade loops
and swirls, unwinding clarity,
movement, joy. When the divide
between water and air is cold-packed
and unmistakable, forces and states
of being may unite. Undercurrents

of hoeing, hewing, humming.
Ripples of a circumspect gaze.
An ancient corn cob, a dropped
fishing spear, rings fanning
from a cupped palm.

3.

Do giant slushy pops still exist
or have these plastic Slurpee cups
the size of watering cans been rolling
in brush by the skunk cabbage
at the Todmorden Mills wildflower preserve
housing ants, rain, mosquitoes
and spiders since 1982?

4.

The official, thirtyish, bristled chin, wades in,
angling for a grip on the fourth
body this season. *Maybe the poor
chump's better off, you know?* His black
boot, a slime-slick rock, careening and fingers
flung through reedy air. Steady, okay,
wait—two hands holding zippo, *nada*—
Was there a splash? His walkie-talkie's
gone under to join what fell and sank
with buddy from the bridge. Up there,
his partner awaits confirmation,
gloved fingers on the railing, round
black speaker at her ear. Give her
a Luminous Veil. Give her a single
malt, neat. Give her a moment
alone with this feat of engineering
and its larger-than-life legacy.
She wants a word.

5.

I don't know what to tell you
about life along the Don. It troubles me
to imagine its wild, abundant, free-
flowing past, and how the forms of survival
I was taught to practice have left it
like a dirty, sodden rag. The year I was 22
I crossed it twice a day, sometimes more,
by bicycle, subway, streetcar. On foot,
a friend at my side. We were
cub reporters, I'd taken a call, heard
news meant only for me. He unpeeled
me from my desk to walk me home.
I might have looked down as we crossed,
vaguely noted the familiar, brown trickle
in its trench. I didn't think of the Don
as a waterway, a succession of histories,
an altered form. The valley was
forbidding, unknowable; to live on
its eastern flank was to score
an arresting view. That morning
I crossed the river one kind of person;
I returned used-up, hollow, littered
with debris, dismal as the Don
but still moving, this way
and that, without
apparent design, braced
for my own Improvement Plan. I was due
to be channelled and dredged.

6.

Capt. Hugh Richardson's rages and bellows,
caught on a putrid 1834 wind, rising
from the deck of his grounded
vessel at the mouth—
The destroying cancer! Destructive industry!—
still fury and eddy with gull screeches
over the head of a repatriated wood duck
traversing the greasy pools
of Keating Channel. (The captain
curses the Don's impassable silt,
not the tanneries, abattoirs,
paper mills, flour mills, lumber mills,
lantern factories and cattle fields
from which it cascaded.)

7.

Taylor regards the clump
of promising valley clay in his palm.

From the protective shade of oaks,
Simcoe turns his gaze on a stand of pine,
sees masts for ships of war.

Davies takes a pig for a country walk.
Gooderham inspects his windmill's lazily turning blades.
Scadding lays a celery trench, mulches
a bed for tender asparagus shoots.

Gardiner scales a backyard fence to scramble
down the valley. He scrapes his ankles
on raspberry canes, tramples
asters, maps out where
to blast the hill and shove
the river over.

8.

A Rob Ford bobblehead is wedged
in the Y of a staghorn sumac branch
near a patch of graffiti—*I be creepin'*
while you sleepin'—on the underside
of the Dundas Street bridge. The sumac
were planted along the once-bleak bank
by sweat-streaked, jean-clad champions
of native species. How long before a
high wind or passing cyclist knocks
the doll free? Its painted-on eyes,
the rerouted shore: now you
see it, now you don't.

9.

That particular night heron spent
two motionless hours perched on a post
poking through the surface near a crack
in the concrete that encases the lower bank.
Its grey-blue bill trained on water, head feathers
ever-so-slightly rearranged by the breeze. Mourners
in the hundreds were drifting downriver

aboard kayak, canoe, rowboat, raft, reenacting
the Funeral for the Don. The chief keener,
mid-wail, erect in the bow, spotted
the stock-still bird. Fell
mute. The heron's intentions
were clear. People stared. Some leaned
so far over to peer (like the bird)
directly into the stink, their
vessels began to list.

10.

Sauriol's memories waft downstream
from the Forks, interrupting the flow
on the DVP. Nostrils lift,
ears twitch. Vehicles
bob and sway:

the scent of the balm of Gilead—
the sweet tremolo of a saw-whet owl—
the sad trilling of American toads, so plaintive—
dozens of eastern bluebirds dropped
from a sky as blue as their wings—

11.

A dusty labourer from the brickworks,
dragging on a smoke; a boy
felling a cedar for his latest
ingenious lean-to; an afterschool
trio hugging armloads of trilliums;
buddy, down on his luck, come

all the way from Nova Scotia to erect
a sheet-metal shack on the Flats.
This ghostly gang follows the river's
forgotten, curlicue shoreline, seen
only by owls and bats, reminiscing,
foraging, speculating on what's
yet to float their way, or
surge on by.

12.

An empty mickey, lid tight, bobs
and meanders, sunlight pooling
in its thick, clear glass.

A corroded nine-volt settles in silt,
kicking up a tiny, temporary, unseen cloud.

The blackbirds' *conk-la-rees*
ricochet from willow to willow
skipping over a log so tattered and forlorn
it can never have stood and splayed
into branches and offshoots,
bright green leaves.

13.

Ah, here she is, Elizabeth Simcoe's ghost—
she's commandeered an abandoned canoe—
Canada geese are splashing and bathing—
she's giddy with swamp gases,
summoning loons.

14.

A Tyee noses upstream, dodging
cigarette butts, coffee cup lids, Styrofoam
crumbs and shards of iPhone
packaging through waters
too warm and up, at intermittent
weirs, precisely, scientifically
angled ladders.

This singleminded chief of all
salmon no way no how voyageured
from the Pacific to this concoction
of road salt and fertilizer, storm sewer
outflow and emptied toilet tanks
propelled by its own fins. No sir. It was
caught, flown over mountains and prairies,
poured into lake water, transformed
into sport for eager anglers.

Ladies and gentlemen of the post-glacial,
post-agrarian, post-Victorian, post-pastoral,
post-industrial, post-landfill, post-
radical-environmental-activist—
ladies and gents of the new-and-improved,
Better-Homes-and-Gardens era of Don River
restoration, please allow me to further describe
the journey undertaken by this pink-scaled
fish of all fishes. This fish

was not game. This Tyee cruised
Lake Ontario's murk, steering clear
of hooks and bait. It smelled

river. Through the port land's rumbles
and slicks, eroded soil grit and driveway sealer
aroma, through beer cans and algae, rainwater
spiked with goose shit, this fish
heard the Don's muted
cough and reeled

in its current. It swims hard and sure—
it belongs here now, it has thrown itself
on the mercy of these ragged, panting waters—
it aims for the source.

Pacific Ocean Tariffs and Tradeoffs

One tsunami for the bleached corals.
Two thumbs up for the jellyfish apocalypse.
Three rigs capsized on a polystyrene reef.
Four trawlers for a stranded sockeye.

Five barnacled wrecks per algae bloom.
Six lost rowers churning the blob.
Seven referendums on phytoplankton suffocation.
Eight economists crying (acidification).

Nine cruise ships swarmed by selkies.
Ten bitter folk songs 'round a tide pool.
Eleven explorers (drowning myths)
for sea turtles submarining North.

Twelve teeming islands fare-thee-welling.

Life Without Winter

No more blinding
perfection a footprint
could mar. Adios to knee-deep
surrender—glorious, burrowing
thoughts. Forget any sun-
bounced illusion of softness,
reprieve. My grey

coat engulfs me. I play
up the chin-tuck retreat
from fanged wind into
frozen-breath-caked scarf.
These old boots grimace
with salt stains. Toes
mat the fur within.

Everyone jokes
bring on the melt but I won't
betray this sharp, narrow
icicle longing. After
their annual eye-popping
flame-out, maples

gamely hold their
scaly limbs aloft. Remember
laughing, falling backside
into drifts, flapping
arm bones into wings. I see
woodpeckers, dreys and sheers
of nostril-fusing

blue. When I undertake
the slow sacrament of wrapping
my bone-cold self in layers, step
knowingly into the knife-blade
morning, I transform, as
in a painting by Lemieux,
into a figure
risking her life
to pay her respects.

Defeat

I surrender to stop signs,
storms, that loose screw
in the window casing, grime
defiling the grout. I acknowledge
the dissolution of my first love
and that crucial, painful inning
when the visitors' cleanup batter
cracked a drive to deep left,
ran gale-force, slid cleanly
into third. (My tag swept
short, I allow.) I yield
to the forces that stilled
the stunned sparrow we hoped
to rescue. I flailed at make-believe,
tossed up wobbly Kool-Aid
concessions. See me bristle, snap,
critique. I hail the careful ones
who cradle test tubes, resist
the bait, skip the link, tally
data with purity of heart—
and whosoever can be counted on
to name, on sight, amid further
distressing reports, any given
wide-eyed species of owl.
May I fall into their knowing.
I submit to winter's
half-melt shame and kneel
before summer's trumped-up
flames. Lead me, please,
past this wall-pounding cry

for reasons, just desserts, safe
passage to a lost calm. Give
over, make way—I
concede. I concede.

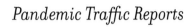

Pandemic Traffic Reports

A Curse on South Keys

Briefly busy on Bronson.
A bit weird on the ramps.

As many as three collisions.
No lingering construction.

Things are heavy from Little Italy to…
about… Maitland. Eastbound,

that's just awful. Oh my
God. Slow, slow,

awful and slow. Right
around, uh, right around…

…what does that
look like to me? Over in

Gatineau today, O
my goodness, really, really

hideous. That seems
like a heck of a

broken down vehicle.
There've been a number of

collisions—close to twenty!
In some places it's a peace

"shuttle" this morning. There Is
No Train. The 417 is wide open

right across the city. Some
sort of curse has befallen

South Keys. You can see
how that kind of rigmarole

can really slow down
traffic. The 50 is a very

grim thing indeed.
Chaudière's busy, but it's

not that gross. There's like
a little Bermuda's Triangle

there, in Blossom Park. Now
that's an intersection every-

body loves. Good
news for Hog's Back

folks. It's not a civil
commuter route, but if you

like taking a look at things, slow—
Even Colonel By

is moving. There's no
traffic right now. You can

go there. That's why
Hallie and I are talking about

chips and pucks. Folks
are being, perhaps, ahem,

a bit careless? All five
bridges are now

wide open. The 417
has been a delightful

nightmare this afternoon.
Watch your step

coming out the front door. *And now,*
Doug Hempstead is here with the traffic

Doug—
Doug…?
Doug?!

Well, no Doug.

The Church That Became a Spa

Eh, none of that, there's
no traffic at all. The Chaudière

Bridge has simmered down. People
are behaving themselves. You might

find yourself in a long lineup
at the drive-through for coffee.

No collisions. People aren't
running into each other

and other things. That's good news
for you *and* the police. No one

wants to get out of their car
this morning. It's bloody

cold out there. It's not
an afternoon for Doc Martens.

You could walk to Southpointe,
but you couldn't really

drive. That's not a good
winter boot at all. Skating

conditions, as of 3:55,
are "fair," they say—

the whole skateway
is open. After coming

around that bend you're
going to stop, right there

on the highway. I mean,
it's stopped. It's just—

stopped. Over in Gatineau
seems the nastiest. Not

sure if that's people
who are freaked out

or stuck behind something
salting the road. Dramatic

slowdowns on chemin Vanier.
Belfast—an eight-car

pile-up. If that's your
route to Ottawa, boy oh

boy, you're not going
to like that. Police in

one direction, gawkers
in the other. The snow

makes things treacherous—
There was a car on its

roof, over by Carling.
There's a berm rising

between the sidewalk
and the road. Just after

the trailer park. Past
the church that

became a spa
that became

a cannabis shop.
As soon as you get

to The Split, you
know that it's on.

My Favourite Stretch of Road

Looks like I'm seeing
a collision. A collision

in Barrhaven. A collision
in Kanata as well. It looks like…

you're approaching…
Hazeldean. But it's

that side street. What's it
called? Near the PetroCan

& the DQ. What once was
a very nice Dodge Ram truck

is no longer. A vehicle
in flames. Yeah, a real

wonderful mess. Ottawa
Police are reporting forty-one

collisions today. From the ramp
for the 5 through Hull. On my

favourite stretch of road
in the whole city. Very grim,

foggy, monochromatic. Between
Lees and Riverdale, both

directions. All the way out
to Montreal Road. Eastbound

174 is grim—
grim, grim, grim. That

sounds like a street name
in Barrhaven. It's closed. And it's

going to be closed
for some time. The canal

is "fair." That's one better
than "poor." I would just

stick it out. "If the big box
stores are not following

protocols I'll come
down on them

like an eight-hundred-pound
gorilla." [Oops. Doug

Ford. Wrong Doug.] They're
asking for patience. If you go

across them, you'll *pshah*—
you'll wonder what I'm

talking about. Keep
your distance. Eastbound 50

is actually improving.
Once you can see the casino

you're out of it. If it were
me, I'd be taking Innis.

That Karaoke Clip

That's curious. It's
usually busy coming *from*

Aylmer. It's the double-fake
by Environment Canada. There's

no snow. It's a nice, bright
afternoon. Just some people

taking the scenic route home
instead of the highway. Everyone's just

chilling out. Good news upon
good news. I had a call

from someone driving in
from Metcalfe. You probably

can't hear him. Not a single
snowflake. I have a snorting

Labradoodle behind me.
The whole canal's classed

"good." He sounds like
a potato in a food

processor. We've had
a really good year

for the canal, even if
you can't eat a Beavertail

out there. According to my daughter,
it's always a little better

than what they say. Even that first
section by the Mackenzie King Bridge—

It's a Friday feeling
out on the roads. I can't be

the only listener
who wants to hear

that karaoke clip again.
It seems to be affecting

the ramp. Shoulda filled
the bird feeders

this morning. It's a cold one.
Icy. Eastbound Walkley,

right near the drive-test
place, where you take

your sixteen-year-old
that terrifying day

they go to get
their license.

Such Wonderful Commutes

Any major route
with half a heart will

tell you: Traffic is great!
You will be smiling so hard

people will be looking at you
like you are crazy. Unless you

like going slow. We're supposed to
have the swing bridge

at Hog's Back reopen
tomorrow, but I don't know

if the odds-makers
are going to touch that. People

are struggling with the zipper
merge. There's lots & lots

& lots of warning
signs that those lanes

are closing. The cones—
the cones make everything

nasty. Even people in
Jeeps are ending up

in the ditch. Make sure
you have more than

your running lights on. The least
safe position you can

be in, folks, is stopped.
You don't want to be

a sitting duck. They teach
that in driver's ed. A bit of

a bugaboo. A visual distraction
just beyond the Tim Horton's. Alan,

I've just been brought a
chicken salad, and now I have

two dogs looking at me
with loving eyes. It's like

a heavy sturgeon all the way
to Bronson. It might become

more than that when they start to
fish the thing out. Traffic pouring in

from the suburbs. Coming
through the trees and approaching

the sportsplex. You're
going to be stopped

from the little church
all the way down

the hill. Across from
the Costco. Over by

Lincoln Fields. Perhaps
down to Manotick

& such. The westbound
417 is busy from Nicholas

to Woodroffe. I had a call
from A, this listener who

I haven't heard from
in ages because he's

had such wonderful
commutes. One, two, three;

four, five, six;
seven, eight, nine—

ten collisions. Eleven.
Twelve—

You'll be getting a long
look at the highway. Just

like the old times. You can
go home and paint it.

You Could Charge Admission

No one is leaving
their house this morning

by the looks of it. There's
nothing sort of freaky

going on. It's overcast,
grey, the same colour

as most of the cars
in this town. Lots of folks

are staying home
to check their plants,

I guess, if they haven't
killed them already

like I have. Those
who are out & about

aren't running into
each other very

very much. People are opting
to take the day off or not

going to school because
of Omicron. It's a bit

busy in Centretown,
though. Busy by

Lebreton Flats. Over
by the war museum, going

both ways, I'm not sure
what's going on. Oh

that's because it's bucketing
down snow in the west

end. The money
people are spending on

windshield washer fluid.
If you can avoid

the section between
Parkdale and Woodroffe,

you're golden. It's pretty
but it's difficult to see. Near

the Tavern on the Green
where you can get

the fancy hot dogs
when it's warm outside—

It's a ring of fire in
that area. In Hintonburg

on the main drag;
Westboro, too. That's

just shopping, it's that
time of year. We have a new

kitten here, Robyn.
How many animals do you

have there, Doug?
Five. *You could charge*

admission. Five animals
and three teenagers. *Don't*

charge admission for
the teenagers. The snow

might be hiding some
slippery spots. Lineups

are still visible outside
the Minto rapid testing kit

site. It was a fierce
afternoon commute. Don't

forget the LRT construction.
I'm not seeing any

people having difficulty
getting where they're

going. It stays fine
right out of town. Not too

shabby at all. The 15-year-old
just got dropped off

at school. My girlfriend
got back & said it's like

a ghost town. Poof—
all that traffic is gone.

The Great Fire of Main-à-Dieu

In June 1976, a wildfire swept through the village of Main-à-Dieu, on the southeastern coast of Cape Breton Island, burning down seventeen family homes—including that of my paternal grandparents—and the gothic, century-old, Roman Catholic church.

The imaginative texts that follow draw on deliberate research, but just as chiefly on stories and anecdotes overheard by my child self, hovering in kitchens on the fringes of adult conversation, and also on rumours and memories shared with me directly, intermittently, over several decades.

Conflagration Season

As spring sparks, I crouch, lie low.
Black spruce gather in my ash.
Mosses hint of afterglow.

The torch's light was mine to bestow.
Whose fury restores the berry patch?
Absorbing spring, I crouch, sink low.

Over grasslands I might shriek and blow,
up mountain ranges seer and slash—
these mosses harbour an afterglow

reeking of peat and snowmelt woe.
Combustion's a cinch: ignition, flash.
Delighting in spring, I crouch, lie low.

Transforming remnants to fuel's slow
work. I'm gathering kindling for my stash.
Spring's ablaze. I crouch, lie low.
Mosses smoulder in afterglow.

Chowder Day at the Grey Seal Café

Some days it's out of my head.

I'm down to the café for a bowl.
I don't normally pay it any mind,
that picture from the paper, the old
church: what was left of it, like
they were only just putting it up,
still had to get to the walls.

> *Me and Clare, we come up with*
> *this plan. Wrestle coyotes. Stalk*
> *lynx. Lock eyes with some scared-shitless*
> *deer, all that crap. You know*
> *where the rabbits hide? Afternoon*
> *that never ends, slingshot*
> *off the workbench, swipe*
> *the bologna (just in case),*
> *matches from the drawer.*

Ma's heart—that church
was where they laid her mother out,
and her sister Lillian, and Uncle Rory
who had to be pulled from the water.
They'd lay them and leave them
alone in the night. They had God,
Ma said, and some were so
old or mean they really did
have no one else.

We run—our feet suck down
in the sponge. Splashes of strawberries: drops
from a bleeding cut. The poplar leaves
dry, like paper. Huge pot on the flame
and me stirring. Like Dad in the trawler,
bubbling and splattering, sleeves up his elbows.
Weeks on end, he's gone. He's the one
who says run your finger over
the Holy Ghost and taste. They calls this
angelica. (Them flowers are
right sugary, aren't they?)

That spring was so strange to us,
who weren't meant for the heat. No way
we had a big pot like that, angelica's
barely out in June. But we made
a team, me and Clare, like Dad and Horse
sweating on those massive boats,
and side-by-side on the crew
afterward, to pull it

down, ashy steeple
and all. The blackened beams
look holy to me, blessings
drifting and settling in all
the open spaces. There's old
Horse himself, at his table
in the corner. (*Murdock*, he's baptized,
imagine that.) Horse

has the chowder too,
everyone knows when Janie's
got a pot on. He's slurping,

he's nodding, he's Clare's
father, soft as butter, never
too hard on us, maybe not
hard enough—he's caught me
stuck on that photo. It's not

a smile exactly but his eyes
sorta say, it's long past, it's over, quit
thinking it through. Forty years,
this day. *Just kids* is what's
in his eyes. Then

it flares, even he
can't douse it. *Which one
struck the match?* I get up
and pay Janie and get
the hell out.

The Coyote, the Turtle and the Plover

(or misadventures during Sunday mass)

For their final hurrah, the rafters
inhale *Almighty*. Let go
amen, amen. Fingers
tapping pews, minds float
toward turnips and beer. A twitch
in the moss on the rise. Coyote brakes,
paws half-sunk, nose tweaked.

Over Bakeapple Bob's bog gone dry,
that creature Aloysius let get away:
plodding, teetering, heaving
its shell. Onward. Seaward. A
mumble, a ripple, a lurch: the peat
puffs a plume. Spits a spark.
Bakeapple's axe head wobbles.
Turtle's leatherhead tilts.

Across the way's our outrageous collection of sand,
constructed from skeletons, wrack and silk. There! One shy
plover's twig legs flash—
licks of orange. Has anyone ever
spied a nest? No more of this

undercover houha: away we go,
gusting through beach grass,
smoking the blades.

Father D's Trinity Sunday Sermon,
Hours Before it Struck

They don't say
nothing in The Acts
about the pain you'd
put up with. Holy spirit
dropping atop your head
like that. *Cloven tongues
like as of fire.* We're talking God
boring a hole through your skull
to the folds where your soul's
tucked away. That's right. This ability
to preach to the far corners
so any wanderer could
understand—you wouldn't
obtain such a gift without cost.
This is what I impress
upon them. Let's go, people
of the late 20th Century. Doing your duty
by God won't protect you. Men
of motorized boats what need
painting and cross-eyed children who
sit right close to hear the stars
through static. Longhaired boys
who hitch rides into Sydney on Saturday
and slink into pews on Sunday. Mothers
who lash wet jeans in fog to the line
and young women who forego
the mores and undergarments

of previous generations. Open your
arms, your hearts,
your mouths. Prepare (I can't
help myself, I do
get carried away with
the Pentecost) to melt.

"Like Big Sea Waves Rolling
Through the Woods"

The fire headed with gathering menace
toward the tidy village, burning on a
five-mile front. Midnight, militia,

firefighters from all nearby
communities. Wind dropped, air
cooled. It settled

in a swamp. Beaten. Sunday,
a hotter day. Mass at Immaculate Conception Church
—since 1883, far out to sea, fishermen

could see its spire. High
80s, sunny skies, bone-dry forest.
Wind. West. Flames swept

the hills, the magnificent
Gothic church. The proud white
steeple fell. *It happened so*

fast. Father Dolhanty moved
swiftly among the stricken. Uncle Tom,
his home gutted. Smoke inhalation. Burns

on his back. *They pushed me*
into the car to get away. It moved
erratically, levelling several in a row,

jumping the road. Fishing boats
reduced to skeletons. All they could do
to stay one step ahead. Everything

except the clothes on her back.
Weeping, staring. *We looked
out the window and ran*

for our lives. Rainfall, brief, twenty-four
hours too late. The fire
burned its

way to the sea.
Murdock, Ambrose, Johnny, Neil, Mike, Elias, Bob—
all their homes had gone.

Horse with Lawn Ornaments at the Scene

That Jesus H. photo in the Post.
Fists in my pockets, watching it go.
T-shirt and shorts, my gut to the flames
like a dinner roast. Here's how
I recall it: Maime and the boy, we're in
the truck, stuck at the roadblock, smoke
licking the taillights. She's gripping
my shirt, *fuck, the house—*
The boy whimpers. Buddy won't
let us through. Right full of himself.
Off-limits, he says. *Back
the way you came.* Hooks a thumb
in his belt. So I got flames

in my eyeballs, molten beams,
eating up baseboards, wallpaper, shingles.
The siding drips, the frame is bones,
the windows (holes now) belch
and roar. A thousand nails
glowing. Our two mini racers
rear and neigh from their positions
in the grass. (Just mown with the rider
that went up with the shed.) Finally
got something to whinny over. They call me

Horse. I'm hefty, gentle
& quick. *He'd eat a whole carrot
right outta your hand.* Made the boy
laugh. His room lit up first: paper
planes & comics. Maime liked to say

I'm no Clydesdale, just an old pony.
I carved them for Christmas: that woman
sure loved her trinkets. It rushed
the screen door like a long-lost
child. Shoulda tossed them
in the truck (they were too
hot to touch).

Bird's Eye View

Lucy Mountain of Wadden's Lane reports
the cawing turned her head: a telltale
silhouette atop a spruce in the ditch.
The tree was one of a few still standing
that far up the road, branches burnt to nubs,
bark black as crow. The bird's teardrop shape
on that distant branch Lucy took as a sign
the fire was out this time for real. But mercy,
the racket. And that charred, lonesome
spruce. Like a ghost, she said. A ribbon
of cinders. She couldn't help hearing those
caw-caw-caws as a soul calling out. *Anguish*
is a word she used. Alarm, alarm, alarm.

*

The barn swallows huddled in the eaves
at Elias Gallant's have welcomed refugees: the flapping
and rustling have increased tenfold. *You wouldn't
believe the commotion up there*, Elias writes.
The cheeping commences at 4 a.m. When
Elias leaves for the wharf they attack
from the lintel, *chureee!* Bombs
away. Elias believes the birds are trying
to put out the fire. They make him
think of water bombs, which he wishes
had tumbled by the dozen out of helicopters
that awful Sunday. No one can fathom
the ministry's reasoning. Main-à-Dieu wasn't
worth saving, we suppose. That burnt

smell that singes your nose with every breath
has the swallows on high alert. The very air
is infused with disaster. Anything
in motion is a threat.

*

Flossy Hart takes comfort
in the yellow-rumped warbler
frequenting the windowsill of the government-issue
trailer she and her husband and the three
children still home have moved into since
their own house smoked and roared and collapsed
in a fury out of all proportion with the quiet
lives contained within. It was only two rooms,
how much drama can one family fit
in a kitchen with a bed shoved in the corner?
The albums were destroyed but Flossy
was never one to sit sulking. She's embarked
on a new collection: Polaroids of the chip-chipping
bird. (The camera was donated. She won it
in the draw.) "I swear it poses," Flossy writes.
"Cocks its little head, gives me the eye. Even
Ambrose says that bird has a mind
to cheer us up." *Bird's Eye View*
wishes the warbler luck.

*

Murdock Flyn can't sleep. He's taken
to walking Sandy Beach, picking his way
around the kitchen tables and televisions
people hauled through beach grass, hoping
the flames would steer clear. But who
wants a TV set with no house? That terrible
image of Murdock watching it burn, the place
he built himself, on page one of the *Cape Breton Post*,
hands at his sides like clumps of newspaper,
glowing before the heat. His son,
you've all heard by now, was in the woods
with that Gallant boy in the hours before
the fire came to life. *Snaring rabbits*,
they said. Take heart in the thought
of Murdock (you may know him as Horse)
striding the shore, loose jacket flapping—
those fists shall follow me to my grave—
where black-backed gulls, Murdock reports,
in the night that maws before the dawn,
comb the shoreline with unusual intensity,
driving away the herring gulls for no
infraction he can fathom. The plovers, normally
so timid, pay him no mind. They streak
along the tideline like sparks. Harmless
sparks. Murdock emphasizes the adjective.

*

Father Edgar Dolhanty crept into the cemetery
to inspect the safe, which he'd shoved and rolled
out the church door and down the hill just in time
to save the records: nearly a hundred years
of births, marriages and deaths. The weight
of that safe! And the state of old Father Edgar! A true
case of adrenaline transforming into power a man
didn't know he had. Father E insists it was God's
grace come down upon him, and I suppose
that comes into play. Could they be
one and the same, adrenaline and grace?
In the cemetery, a young bald eagle, speckled brown,
was perched atop the lock on the safe, enjoying
his midday meal. A good-sized crab,
shell bits flying. Father paused
with a hand on Eliza Campbell's tombstone,
the one that leans left toward that chipped
statue of Mary like a girl whispering
to her sister in the pew. That majestic bird
eyed the priest with a fierceness that sent him
right back in to dress for evening mass—what
mass we can manage in the musty hall, with no
chairs or hymnals. It was only two o'clock
but the heavy fabric enfolding his arms
and waist calmed him. He was so grateful
to Esther Gallant. She saw those flames
gunning for the church, ran in, grabbed
a massive armload of chalices and vestments,
stuffed them in the trunk of her car. Father's robes
are rumpled now, even torn here and there, but
so what? A servant of the Lord, that one,
a bonafide Mary Magdelene.

Katie Gallant, 5,
of Main-à-Dieu Road, asked
her mother Esther to write in about
the shags. She saw twelve
in a row on the back of Nanny's
flower-embroidered couch, hanging
their oily wings out to dry. Katie
asks, *Do those shags think
Nan's couch is a rock?* I doubt it,
Katie, dear. If it's convenient and dry,
it's all the same to a shag.

*

Ambrose Hart nearly had his head
taken off by a great blue heron
coming in for a landing in that frog pond
down in front of Ambrose & Flossy's.
What *was* Ambrose & Flossy's. Flossy
didn't call this one in herself: she isn't
sure Ambrose saw what he says
he saw. He was in none too good shape
the morning before the fire nor
the next day by the smouldering pit
refusing to move, though Flossy's sure
his supply of rum must've vanished
with everything else. That's how fast
the fire moved through. *Poof!* It turned
her world to dust. No, it weren't Flossy.
Ambrose called me himself. In a clear voice,
clear enough, anyway, he told me he felt

the breeze in his scalp as the heron
swept past. A claw brushed his
thick black hair. It's not unusual
for herons to swoop low over
Ambrose's house and alight in that pond
to hunt bullfrogs and muskrats, tiptoeing
like they can't stand getting their feet
wet, looking like some grim creature
come down to us from before
fire or light was invented. Ambrose guesses
the bird flew lower this time. With the house
gone, it maybe didn't see him, or
with his dark, unwashed hair it thought
he was another blackened stump.

Horse's Hearty Caper Welcome

Got a houseful, Moira. We're after breaking
in the new priest. I hauled it out, the old pot—
corned beef & cabbage. You'd agree, no newfangled
concoction beats a proper boiled dinner. That's
the one thing come outta that fire. A pot. Clare
did the chopping. Insisted. He's home, see?
There, with Katie and her little one. Looks
right happy. I know, it's plain how things were
meant to be with those two. I'm glad he's here,
but Jesus, what he's like. Don't trouble myself,
he says. He's establishing—get that, *establishing*—
a smithy. In. My. Shed. And for money? The boy
proposes to fish. Be Russ's helper. Russ's
other helper. Now what will Katie make of that?
Look at them, shaking hands. Do the others

feel it, I wonder, like a shadow's floated over us all?
The seal hunt. That's his latest. A sin, he calls it. We
owes them. What, pray tell, could I owe a seal? I mean to ask
Father Frank about that. (He comes from fishing folk, too.)
The screams outta them kids! Took a right shine to our
Clare. I should round them up. I keep telling myself
you won't get up from the meal, open your mouth
and usher the sky and all the heavens into the room
on the soft, clear current of your voice. You'd gone
peaceful, cheerful even, that's what I told Clare,

a miracle it was, no more talk of beforetimes,
the old house. Rest easy, my dear. I keeps
your sorrow close. The anger too. He don't

need to hear it. Being away—I hoped
it might calm him. Is it his fault
he could never leave well enough
alone? I can't hardly bring
myself to call them in.

Russell's Deliberation

I can hear him now, whingeing over
every goddamn trap he's gotta haul. Telling me
to Jesus Christ switch why don't I
to the metal kind. He'll court misery, curl up
in the stern nibbling crackers, take an hour
to band a claw. He'll need wake-up calls. Whimper
when the weather's off. Say he doesn't

want to die out there. *At 5 a.m.,*
out there—Russell waves at the waves
that have been there all his life, rolling
over his thoughts, so subtle and constant a motion,
a hum, an endless and varying score, he can't
imagine (or even think to try) what life
away might consist of—

I bring you aboard, there'll be no carrying on
about that fire. I won't stomach it.

That? Honest to God, Russ. Done like dinner.

So Clare wants to fish. Give him
a chance, he says. The West isn't how
it's cracked up. *Total devastation. You wouldn't*
credit it. And the bars. Soul-polluting. Don't
get me started. That's some

nerve he's got. The question is,
the question's always, what would Elias do?
I can hear him now: *I got my own ideas
what was wrong with the West.*

Yeah, Dad, me too. But you know
Clarence. The bugger won't give up.

Lucy Speaks for Walter

Clarence, dear, why dredge
all that up? It weren't *your* fire
smoked out my dear Walter's
lungs. You know how many
fires he tackled? It were his
job. And he loved it. He was
with Parks. Had all the fancy
training and what-not. Ma was
at the Fortress too, brewing vats
of chowder big enough to swim in.
Yeah. Arms like a wrestler's—
the kneading. They still make loaves
like boulders, 18th-century-style.
The pay's worse, benefits
ancient history. Away

long as you been, you don't know
the half of it. I'll tell you what
Walter told me. *Lucy*, he says—
this were years later, right
out of the blue—*it were that hot,
I'd bet that fire started on its own.*
Nonsense I said. But he were
right serious, had this look
he used to get. I've been reading up
since Walter's passing. Ever

hear tell how fire goes
under? Lives on roots and pops
up a field or forest away. Even after

months, after snow. How can such a creature
be conquered? Now they drive
water poles down deep. Back then…
Listen dear, Walter was convinced

your campfire what got
out of hand never did burrow
like they said. No way it snuck
from your yard below the road
and into the bush where
the wildfire really got
going. It got put out
and that was that. *Supposing
the next day a lightening bolt,
just supposing,* he says,

*flicked a dry, dead spruce
like a match.* Walter fought
that fire. I'll tell you what
he told me. It weren't musky
like long-sunken matter
bubbled up from the bog,

blazing back to light—
no, it were flashy and fresh,
wind and oxygen and surrendering
spruce boughs, high-pitched
poplar screams—*A sky fire,
straight from God himself. Nothing
to do with them boys.*

Oral Testimony Pertaining to the
Great Fire of 1976

They say it were two kids playing with matches in the woods.
I know who, alright. Just young, they were. The amount of
furniture that got piled on them tennis courts! We was doing
OK with it till the ministry stepped in. Had a handle on it, we
did. You know people came and took stuff, don't you? Looters.
I wouldn't lie to you, now. From nearby villages. From Sydney.
People were some mad over the blockade. What right did they
have telling us we couldn't come in and save our own homes?
People figured it'd be safer there, with just the field around it,
you know. No trees. Maybe it's true. I don't know. It were awful
dry that month. God knows. The whole place still smouldering
and they went straight for the beach and took what they could
carry. Imagine. The government came in and rebuilt all the
houses. Took their sweet time about it, too. But soon as the
Gallant's fancy yellow sofa turned up—it were lumpy mind
you and awful hard to get out of once you was in it, but they
was so proud of it—soon's the boys thunked it down on the
court—that fire let go the two houses it had in its teeth and
leapt clear across the road. Walter's father's truck died just
as the fire come out of the ditch, heading straight for him
up the centre of the road. It were just one company got all
the rebuilding contracts. Right fishy if you ask me. You do
know Lucy lost a baby, don't you? Not in that fire. One of
'em waltzed right into Elias's front room without so much
as a how d'you do and marched off with his TV. Flossy's new
house, now. They put that up backwards, didn't they? Pounced
right atop that old couch and caught everything around it,
too. Cookstoves and chairs and supper tables. Had the front

door coming straight out the master bedroom. I know who done it, too. Oh no, I won't say. That were a long time ago. That were a bad business. Whose pockets do you suppose got lined for that? In a house fire. Years before. Terrible tragedy that was. The fire was trailing off on the asphalt but it veered back to the ditch, flared up again, and turned back up the road. Straight for Walter's father and his truck. At least one guitar. That belonged to Ambrose, god bless him. Buddy did the designs all wrong. Had to take it down and start over, didn't they? It kept dipping over the side of the road for fuel. As if it knew. As if it had a plan. Some went to stay with family in Ontario or out west. A few just stayed away. You can imagine how she felt not knowing where her kids were that day. Well the government provided trailers, see? Some people never bothered with a house after that. A few months later, the new church was half built. One day, poof, it lit up like a firecracker. They had to start all over again. He got her going, but not for long. Had to leave the truck behind and run for it. The baby's buried here in the cemetery. Little white stone. Anything mighta woken that beast. Cigarette tossed out a car window. Lightning. Sparks off a truck. Or they never could decide on coming home. Same difference, really. They were safe enough, down at their Nan's, but how were she to know?

Incineration of Immaculate Conception Catholic Church (June 6, 1976)

Testimony of volunteer firefighter Walter Mountain

A craze in the air. We seen it
when the truck took the hill
down the shore. The sound of it
like a freight train coming. With
the trees so high you couldn't
tell how close. A crown fire. Lights
up the canopies, tosses cinders
like confetti over shingles,
trailers, boats. We were stood there

before the glebe house. The heat
got right intense, completely
beyond. I yelled
with all that was in me
over the roar and I don't
give a rat's arse who
knows it: we
ran. The house
combusted. She just

went up. Sparks
showered the steeple. The bell
dropped. Not a soul
inside. Luck or the good
Lord's graces? Fire like that
you want lookouts, helicopters. *Non-stop*

communication. Incredible, really, a fire
like that and no one killed.

Testimony of volunteer firefighter Elias Gallant

I keep wondering was it
our fault or we needed
more pressure or the pump
just wore clean out, or what?
It come to us secondhand, like,
the hoses and the lot.

Find a source, turn
the sucker on. The tide
was low, the brook shallow
all that spring. A dry season,
brittle—the steeple
crackled and smoked, we
pumped and sprayed—damn

water wouldn't reach it. I
rushed over the beach to
shut her down—the pump
—ran my tail off amid
the thundering—the smoke
went right like a mug of rum
to me head. The shoreline
exploded, flames and tide
colliding. I blinked,

it vanished. I swears
I heard that bell, clear as Sunday.

A seal swam up, two boys
hauling a couch, fella with a
big-ass TV on his head
like a basket of fruit—

I waved my arms
and hollered—*Get your foolish
arses away from here*! It was raining
ash, spears of grass
ghosted before my eyes.

*Testimony of Esther Gallant, librarian, Foghorn editor,
local archivist*

It lit the tower like a wick.
I ran from the car and grabbed
the first things to hand, Father's
vestments what he'd only taken
off an hour before, the chalices
wiped clean. Flames roaring and Ma
from the back seat *Jesus Mary and Joseph
get yourself back here! If God's after
them things, it's no place of yours
to interfere.* Leave it to Ma
to shout a coherent sermon
in a crisis. I willed

the water from the hoses
higher. Those flames blasted
straight from darkness, I believe that,
I do—all the starved, afflicted,
displaced—this island's black heart

cut loose. You heard tell of our
Irish ancestors? Supposed
criminals. Shipped here and shoved
overboard at Convict's Point. It were
late in the season, see? The captain
wouldn't risk the St. Lawrence
in winter. Imagine the ice
on those rocks. Those what didn't perish
cut their limbs so bad, bloody
torrents streamed into the sea.
Rightfully, this whole enchanted isle
belongs to the Mi'kmaw, not that
too many here give a blessed
reverie to that. Right. The burning

steeple. Our angelus bell
wilted and warped, its rope
coiling to the frayed end the boys
would grip in red-raw palms, leaping
and swinging (our Russell too),
thighs squeezed and ankles
hooking the rough cord, that riotous
peeling up the harbour,
down the shore—

every day, let me tell you,
that gift of feeling up nor down
never mattered, not who built
boats or survived on lobster rolls—
only pale bodies peeling
the song from the bell's hollow,
a wondrous nothingness
now gone. After

the bell went, every
square inch of that church
acquiesced. Pillars writhed, pews
bottomed out. Heat slunk
through the cushion floors
to the softwood planks beneath.
My dear, those flames lapped the blood
on God's forehead, the cold sweat
and bitter vinegar, enveloped

the weeping virgin. I think on
the shattered windows, all
those years of gleaming
while we prayed. That bell
had proper godparents, you know.
It anchored us. It summoned us
in luxurious notes. It offered
in its swaying, in its glint and its swell,
in the sureness of its clamour
and the hush that followed
its thrice daily outbursts, glory
enough and awe aplenty,
shelter for our souls.

Flossy Baking Bread

Moira was after calling me
a saint. Two loaves in the oven, two
in the works. *Go on*, I said. It's just
a thing needs doing. But oh my God
the heat. Kneading on a day like
that. Nothing much on the CB. Sunday.
Between crackles the odd *How now
buddy! Skipping the mass again, eh?* We sat
with our cups, glad for the quiet. The men
what couldn't fish were in from church,
waiting on their dinner. Ambrose might
or might not come up. Down there
since Friday. His chickens needed feeding.
I shook my head when Moira asked. He gets this
look on his face like no man woman or child
would begrudge him. Once I took
a sip. Burnt a hole in my heart. Moira
was off home. Horse done the cooking,
he liked to on Sundays. She was only
gone a minute. I stood there pressing
the dough. Fog, I thought. The window
looks in back (I should say *looked*)
toward the swamp. People say they
sensed it coming. But no fog ever rolled in
that fast. How'd I wind up right smack
in it, out in the yard, squeezing St. Ann
in my palm? Four loaves. A morning's
work. Ambrose hobbled out,
squinting and waving.

Tally

Bedframes, pillows, sheets. The matches
and scribblers by the lamps. Bulbs screwed
in tight. Each hammered nail and board, hard-won
tins of tobacco, golden packets of Vogue
cigarette papers, ceilings staring down
through a sad yellow tinge. That gummy corner
that no mop could reach. The stove
and each bread pan stored underneath.
Pantries stocked with sardines, tubs
of corned beef. Pounds and pounds of it
(the flour). Live yeast and turnips eaten up
with salt shakers and decks of cards. A mug
for the 1968 Bateston Baseball champs
and two tiny silver spoons from the Empress
that time Cousin George drove west. A month,
it took, with breakdowns and what
have you. He couldn't give a soul a coherent
reason why. Teddy bears. Shoeboxes stuffed
with photographs and postcards. A town's worth
of St. Anns and St. Judes in cheap metal
on chains. It was a new kind of stew, simmering
down to bewilderment and ash. And what's more—
what Lucy told me she'd think for years
heading home from delivering the mail—
the welcome sight of the clean white
house with blue trim amid spruce
on the hill as she rounded
the bend before driving down
to the shore. All 84 hens
got from Alec. Their coop.
The spruce on the hill.

Songs for Main-à-Dieu

Russell's Hymn

We slouched through mass sure it was dead,
them blazes done dancing branch to branch.
Clarence in the choir mouthing *holy fuck*.
Old Father D off key.

Smoke out the duck blind, cough up the shore.
Kick up some ashes and tears.
This is the day of embers and blame.
Round up your girls and boys.

I caught sparks in my open palm—
fireflies burst from the bush. Our own
house popped and sizzled and Mom
stood and stared the flames down.

I'll go on filling buckets, my Lord,
till Catalone Lake's puckered dry.
You dropped this ferment atop my head.
How can I tamp it down?

Where the Drunken Herring Swirl

To Scaterie we bob, we float
We who make the crossing gloat
And chug our rum
Till the fear's gone numb

Play a jig on a sweet-talking fiddle
To merry us through the tiddle

Grey seals whip up the tide
Rock-and-roll us wondrous wide
For their home on Hay to hide
We'll tack, skim, skirr and glide

For a jig on sweet-talking fiddle
Might merry us through the tiddle

Out where drunken herring swirl
Our fisher folk a-twirl
Till through the chop they're hurled
And all their dreams unfurl

But a jig on a sweet-talking fiddle
Will merry us through the tiddle

Janie and the Selkies

I married a quiet man.
No carrying on, no drunken sprees.
How to assess where things stand?
He sketches lichens, sickly trees.
Plunks down before some flower.
Disappears for hours.

>When selkies sing, their harmonies bring
>me beside myself down to the wharf.
>I'll be out there pacing the wharf.

I don't like this situation,
can't tell if he's okay.
I'm running low on patience.
When I'm down to the café,
pouring coffee, serving toast,
they'll be out around the coast

hauling traps and banding claws
as if the coast is clear. But
I see scowling waves and rocks,
ancient selkies drawing near.
How can I pin down the flaws—
picture the ocean's widening jaws—

in this plan when I hardly know
what's got this man so sure
he should let his trusted helper go,
and embark on this detour?
The ingredients aren't right.
When I think of all that might

go wrong, and Clare the one at his side?
Hardly knows a boat from a truck.
Suppose it turns rough in the tide?
Now they've entwined their luck
again—it went so poorly before,
why is he back for more?

> When the selkies sing, who will I bring
> with me down to the wharf?
> I'll be out there pacing the wharf.

"Ice-Age Surprise": In 2007, the sons of Yuri Khudi, a Nenets reindeer herder, found a nearly intact mammoth carcass on the banks of northern Siberia's Yurebei river. Called Lyuba, after Khudi's wife, she represented, at the time, the most complete fossil of a prehistoric creature ever found. Her discovery is tied to climate-change-induced permafrost melt. I saw Lyuba at the Royal B.C. Museum in 2016 and found the book *Mammoths: Giants of the Ice Age*, by Adrian Lister and Paul Bahn, invaluable.

"Pandemic Traffic Reports": These are collages made up of fragments from live broadcasts by Doug Hempstead, CBC Radio Ottawa's traffic reporter, who delivered his cheerful, animated reports from a makeshift home studio throughout the pandemic.

"Don River, Crossings and Expeditions": Section 1: Influential Toronto-area conservationist Charles Sauriol wrote two popular books about life at his cottage at the Forks of the Don. Elizabeth Simcoe's diary, published in 1934, chronicled colonial life in Upper Canada, including the Don Valley's flora and fauna. Section 2: The area currently known as the Don Valley was historically farmed by Indigenous communities, and its lower river called, in Anishnaabemowin, Wonscotonach. Section 5: The 1886 Don Improvement Plan is discussed in Jennifer Bonnell's "Imagined Futures and Unintended Consequences: Toronto's Don River Improvement Project, 1880-1910." Section 7: William Taylor was one of the three Taylor brothers who founded the Don Valley Brick Works in 1889. William Davies was proprietor of William Davies Co. Pork Packing Plant. Gooderham and Worts, famed distillers, began in the early 1830s with a large windmill near the mouth of the Don. John Scadding grew orchards, fields of rye and barley, asparagus, celery and "melons of all kinds" on his early-nineteenth-century Don Valley homestead (*Landmarks of Toronto*, John Ross Robertson, 1984). Frederick G. Gardiner, chair of Metropolitan Toronto from 1953-1961, by his own account, scrambled through the valley, in and out of backyards, to prove his engineers wrong that there was no room for a highway. "We'd have a look and say, 'We'll move the river over. We'll tear down a hill.'" ("Tracing the Social and Environmental History of the Don River," Jennifer Bonnell, Don River Valley Historical Mapping Project.). Section 9: A "Funeral for the Don" a street-theatre/protest march held in Toronto in November, 1969, featured Elizabeth Simcoe as a character. Section 10: Italicized text is from Charles Sauriol's *Tales of the Don*. Section 14: Lake Ontario is stocked with Pacific salmon (for catch-and-release anglers) by the Ontario Ministry of Natural Resources. In the mid-1990s, the Chinook, or Tyee, began migrating up-river each fall.

The Great Fire of Main-à-Dieu: Anecdotes and "testimony" incorporated into these poems are the true property of relatives and locals who shared their fire memories, including my late father; several aunts, uncles and cousins; Eric Lahey; the late, formidable Mary Price; Carter Stevens (who fought the fire); Arlene King, Florence Flander; my nanny Beatrice (Wadden) Lahey; my second cousin Nicholas Whalen; and his mother Wendy Whalen. Character names are fictional, but not without geographic relevance: some are popular regional names, and several correspond to names listed in Main-à-Dieu historic census documents. The Grey Seal Café is inspired by the real-life Big Wave Café. "Like Big Sea Waves Rolling Through the Woods" is a found poem compiled from news reports in the *Cape Breton Post* and the *Halifax Chronicle-Herald*, June 7-8, 1976. "Horse with Lawn Ornaments at the Scene" is based on a photo in the *Cape Breton Post* (June 7, 1976), which featured my great-uncle Mike Wadden. Other sources include: the Cape Breton public library's vertical files; the Main-à-Dieu Fishers' Museum; the Beaton Institute at Cape Breton University; the *Louisbourg Seagull*; *Cape Breton Magazine*; *With Changing Tides: The Struggles, Strengths, and Successes of our Coastal Communities*, by Leona (Lathigee) MacNeil; *Awful Splendor: A Fire History of Canada*, by Stephen J. Pyne; *Burning Down the House: Fighting Fires and Losing Myself*, by Russell Wangersky.

There's no question that, the year of the Main-à-Dieu fire, the weather was uncharacteristic for the season and region. It was one of many wildfires blazing in the area, in fact. In not-yet-summer, on what is typically an urelentingly damp coast. Set against the extreme weather systems in our world today, it was an incident that may now seem quaint. But even that relatively modest fire's touch remains potent. A creative work such as this represents one kind of aftermath—the long reach of disaster.

ACKNOWLEDGEMENTS

Heartfelt thanks to all the editors of the publications in which earlier versions of these poems appeared: *The Malahat Review* ("Ice-Age Surprise," as "Permafrost Releases Ice-Age Fossil"), *Literary Review of Canada* ("Urgent Interspecies Telepathy in a Sunlit Bedroom"), *The Walrus* ("Defeat" and "Conflagration Season"), *The New Quarterly* ("Birds' Eye View"), *Arc Poetry Magazine* ("Russell's Hymn," "Horse With Lawn Ornaments at the Scene," "The Coyote, the Turtle and the Plover"), *The Fiddlehead* ("Chowder Day at the Grey Seal Café," "Father D's Trinity Sunday Sermon, Hours Before it Struck," "Lucy Speaks for Walter.") "Salish Sea (with Crows)" appeared (as "Residual") in *Refugium: Poems for the Pacific* (ed. Yvonne Blomer, Caitlin Press, 2017). "Birds' Eye View," inspired by Bill Bussey's bird column in the *Louisbourg Seagull*, was in the chapbook, *Between the Lines* (Banff Centre Winter Writers Retreat, 2017). Poems from "The Great Fire of Main-à-Dieu" appeared in the chapbook *The Great Fire of Main-à-Dieu* (ed. Karen Schindler, Baseline Press, 2020). They are also excerpted (and the section's preface adapted) from the graphic novel-in-verse *Fire Monster* (Palimpsest, 2023), a collaboration with artist Pauline Conley.

"Don River: Crossings and Expeditions" and "A Pair, Fishing the Humber" were written for Lost Rivers guided walks in Toronto. "Don River" also appeared in Newpoetry.ca, the Gesture Press chapbook *Reading the Don*, and in the anthology, *Sweet Water: Poems for Watersheds* (ed. Yvonne Blomer, Caitlin, 2020). Excerpts from "Don River" were included in the 2015 Pan Am Path Poetry Walk, and the 2019 Toronto Biennial of Art. I am indebted to my fellow river poets, and to Helen Mills of Lost Rivers and John Wilson of the Take Back the Don Task Force.

For gifts and offerings too numerous to itemize, I offer heaps of gratitude to John Barton, Jacqueline Best, Yvonne Blomer, Lesley Buxton, Sherry Coffey, Pauline Conley, Moira Dann, Moira Farr, Alyse Frampton, Bethany Gibson, Anne Glover, Luke Hathaway, Jon Hayes & Jen Barratt (& the High Park Nature Centre), Craig Hiebert, Matthew Holmes, Monique Holmes, Steph Khoury, Chris Knight, Wendy Lahey, Dilys Leman, Una McDonnell, Molly Peacock, Rob Taylor, Joan Thomas, Paul Tyler, Rob Winger, Deanna Young, Xiaomin Yu. I'm also grateful to the Inconvenients in Toronto and to the Sun Room poets in Victoria.

Simon Dardick, Jen Varkonyi and the team at Véhicule are my heroes. There is no way to properly thank my longtime editor and friend Carmine Starnino. Quite simply, without him (and his care for poetry, not just my own), I would be lost.

To Sean Howard and Lee Anne Broadhead in Main-à-Dieu, I am grateful for your friendship; your efforts to gather local oral histories; for cozy meals and heartening discussions on literature, culture, politics and more. To my Cape Breton family— especially Bill, Karen, Shawn, Rena, Lil, Angus, Valerie, Charlie, Herman; my late father Sandy Lahey; and his cousin Ray Lahey, also late, keeper of the turtle tale and so many other stories (of questionable degrees of veracity, but so what?)—and to Ray's daughter, Raylene, I thank you all for your parts in granting me this east-coast place of belonging.

The men (and the cat) in my household seem, thank God, not to mind having a poet in their midst. All my love to Henry and Tom; and a slow (sadly ineffectual) blink to Milli.

Talya Rubin • Richard Sanger • Stephen Scobie
Peter Dale Scott • Deena Kara Shaffer
Carmine Starnino • Andrew Steinmetz • David Solway
Ricardo Sternberg • Shannon Stewart
Philip Stratford, trans. • Matthew Sweeney
Harry Thurston • Rhea Tregebov • Peter Van Toorn
Patrick Warner • Derek Webster • Anne Wilkinson
Donald Winkler, trans. • Shoshanna Wingate
Christopher Wiseman • Catriona Wright
Terence Young